LIBRARI

This book is to be retu
It may be borrowed for

-8 DEC 1989		ESSEX, CM8 2AQ
15 JUN 1991	1/10/78	
17 AUG 1991	07 SEP 2001	
25 JUL 1992	17 SEP 2001	
05. 12. 92		
17. 12. 03. 93	2 1 FEB 2011	
17. 05.		

DY28299

DRAMA COLLECTION
MANY LIBRARIES IN ESSEX HAVE
WITHDRAWN FACILITIES FOR EXHIBITIONS AND
18, NEWLAND STREET MEETINGS — ENQUIRE AT YOUR
WITHAM LOCAL LIBRARY FOR DETAILS
ESSEX, CM8 2AQ

Who Calls?

A Play

David Campton

Samuel French – London
New York – Sydney – Toronto – Hollywood

© 1980 BY DAVID CAMPTON

This play is fully protected under the Copyright Laws of the British Commonwealth of Nations, the United States of America and all countries of the Berne and Universal Copyright Conventions.

All rights, including Stage, Motion Picture, Radio, Television, Public Reading, and Translation into Foreign Languages, are strictly reserved.

No part of this publication may lawfully be transmitted, stored in a retrieval system, or reproduced in any form or by any means, electronic, mechanical, photocopying, manuscript, typescript, recording, or otherwise, without the prior permission of the copyright owners.

Rights of Performance by Amateurs are controlled by SAMUEL FRENCH LTD, 26 SOUTHAMPTON STREET, LONDON WC2E 7JE, and they, or their authorized agents, issue licences to amateurs on payment of a fee. **It is an infringement of the Copyright to give any performance or public reading of the play before the fee has been paid and the licence issued.**

Licences are issued subject to the understanding that it shall be made clear in all advertising matter that the audience will witness an amateur performance; that the names of the authors of the plays shall be included on all announcements and on all programmes; and that the integrity of the author's work will be preserved.

The Royalty Fee indicated below is subject to contract and subject to variation at the sole discretion of Samuel French Ltd

> Basic fee for each and every
> performance by amateurs   Code D
> in the British Isles

In Theatres or Halls seating Six Hundred or more the fee will be subject to negotiation.

In Territories Overseas the fee quoted above may not apply. A fee will be quoted on application to our local authorized agent, or if there is no such agent, on application to Samuel Frendh Ltd, London.

ISBN 0 573 13345 X

CHARACTERS

Mrs Abernethy
Cook
Lane
Twilley
Mrs Boone
Intruder

The action takes place in the kitchen of a large Victorian house

Time—night in the late nineteenth century

PRODUCTION NOTE

Although the arrangement of the setting is left to the producer's discretion, it is suggested that the row of bells should be imagined as in the "fourth wall" —so that the characters can see them, but the audience cannot.

WHO CALLS?

The kitchen of a large Victorian house. Night

At the rear is a door opening on to a narrow passage, which leads in one direction to the scullery, and in the other to back stairs going up to the rest of the house. The room is simply furnished with four chairs and a cupboard

It is night. A lamp and candles have been lit, and a red glow suggests a well-stoked range. For all that, the corners of the room are lost in shadow and a blanket of gloom seems to have settled over its occupants. These are Mrs Abernethy, housekeeper, normally possessed of a dignified and lady-like demeanour, but at present slightly out of her depth; Lane, lady's maid, who likes to think of herself as a lady, but whose achievement occasionally falls short of her ambition; Cook, who knows that she is no lady and does not care who else knows it, either; and Twilley, maid of all work, slow, rough and resigned to her lot. The four servants sit solemnly, the silence broken only by a sigh from Cook, a sniff from Twilley and the sound of Mrs Abernethy drumming her fingers on a chair arm. At last Lane speaks

Lane Her jewel box played a tune when it was opened, but the works had run down.
Mrs Abernethy So you remarked.
Lane She sat all a-glitter in front of the great mirror.
Twilley Ah!
Lane Hung about with a lord's ransom.
Mrs Abernethy Locked away now. Listed and locked away.
Lane Necklaces, pendants, brooches: every precious stone she possessed. And her fingers stiff with rings.
Cook (*dryly*) You tell it better every time.
Lane Didn't I find her myself?
Cook Shall we be allowed to forget it?

Lane Even the tiara that hadn't seen Company since her last County Ball.

Cook Whenever that was.

Lane Diamonds and rubies. "Hell's fire, Lane," she'd say. "Purest flames." Though what she meant by that only she knew.

Cook And she'll not be telling us now.

Twilley I heard an owl this afternoon.

Mrs Abernethy A common occurrence hereabouts.

Twilley I spilled the salt this morning—and broke a plate.

Cook Even more common.

Twilley Warnings.

Cook (*scornfully*) After hearing of which the Mistress hurried to adorn herself for one last time.

Lane She'd done it before. Often. "Let me see what I'm worth, Lane," she'd say. "Let me gloat."

Twilley She died sudden.

Cook No more of that.

Twilley Sorry Cook.

Cook All this harping on death.

Mrs Abernethy Hardly avoidable with the midwife upstairs.

Cook Should she have been left alone?

Mrs Abernethy She knows her duties. Only two persons are required for the laying-out. The midwife and ...

Twilley The Mistress.

Lane She'd passed over before I reached her. Staring at herself with dead eyes.

Cook Vanity.

Lane The last light she saw was the sparkle of diamonds.

Cook How did the sinful old creature come by them? What did she do? Where and how often?

Mrs Abernethy That is for her conscience, not ours.

Cook Diamonds and rubies on sticks of fingers.

Mrs Abernethy She was the mistress.

Cook Diamonds and rubies on cobweb hair.

Lane She was very particular about her hair. "Save the combings, Lane," she'd say. "Ice and snow go together."

Cook Diamonds and rubies. Their weight alone was enough to crush her.

Mrs Abernethy The jewelry was irrelevant. According to the doctor a seizure was possible at any time. In his opinion, from the

position of the body, death must have been almost instantaneous.
Cook Struck down in her pride.
Mrs Abernethy I suggest enough has been said on that subject.
Lane She went as she would have wished.
Mrs Abernethy Enough is enough.
Cook She'd hardly have known she was dead.
Mrs Abernethy Enough!
Cook Enough? Are you still in charge, Mrs Abernethy?
Mrs Abernethy Have I been dismissed? Have I handed in my notice? I was housekeeper this morning and I am housekeeper this evening. Just as you are still Cook, Lane still maid and Twilley still . . .
Twilley Bottom o' the heap.
Mrs Abernethy I hope we all know our places.
Cook Does she know hers? Wherever she is?
Mrs Abernethy She remains upstairs until the funeral. Meanwhile this household will run as it has always run—like clockwork.
Cook The mainspring's broke.
Mrs Abernethy Do you suppose so, Cook? The Mistress had only one concern—that when she rang the bell, it was answered.
Lane It was always answered.
Cook Who's going to answer now there's nobody up there to ring?
Mrs Abernethy Your attitude borders on socialism, Cook. I expected a better example. I can only presume the shock has unsettled you.
Cook She's gone, Mrs Abernethy. To glory or otherwise, but she's gone. Howsoever, if you say so, I'll go on listening for that bell.

A bell rings. There is a sudden silence. The quartet looks up involuntarily at the line of bells used for summoning servants

The bell?
Lane In her bedroom.
Twilley What does it mean?
Mrs Abernethy It means the midwife pulled at the bell rope.
Cook Impudence.
Mrs Abernethy The laying-out must have been completed.
Cook What of that?
Mrs Abernethy Her work must be inspected. And, of course, a light is to burn by the body. Constantly. Candles, Twilley.

Twilley Yes'm. (*She fetches candles from a cupboard*)

Cook If the goody needs candles, let her come down for 'em.

Mrs Abernethy Even a midwife has professional pride.

Cook Are we expected to climb stairs at a nurse's bidding?

Mrs Abernethy No, Cook. Not you. Bring the candles, Twilley.

Twilley Up there?

Mrs Abernethy Where else? The water has to be emptied away too. You can bring the pancheon down.

Cook A midwife has arms.

Mrs Abernethy So have I, Cook; but I presume I am not required to fetch and carry. Come, Twilley. (*She takes a lighted candle in its stick from the top of the cupboard*)

Twilley To Mistress?

Mrs Abernethy Why hang back? You weren't afraid of her while she was alive.

Mrs Abernethy goes out with the candle

Twilley Weren't I, though!

Lane If you don't keep close behind, you'll be left in the dark.

Twilley Ooooh!

Twilley scurries out, after Mrs Abernethy, leaving the door open

Cook Door! (*She shuts the door impatiently after Twilley*) Afraid? It takes imagination to be afraid, and she's no more imagination than a turnip. *You're* pale, though, Lane.

Lane The bell. So unexpected.

Cook Did you imagine *her* hand on the rope? Dead men don't walk, and dead women don't ring bells.

Lane She was a woman of character.

Cook A determined old devil, but some deeds are beyond even her. You're all of a quiver. A quick reviver before the others come down. (*She fetches a bottle of brandy and two glasses from a cupboard. She fills the glasses*)

Lane I didn't believe she reached for the bell-rope. But if such a thing were possible . . .

Cook She'd have found a way. I'll grant she had spirit. She was witching men to her bed when other grannies would have been nursing their rheumatics. Ah, her past was as plain as the paint on her face.

Lane If you felt so bitterly towards her, why did you work in this house?

Cook Why did you?

Lane A place is always a place.

Cook Was that all? (*She hands a glass to Lane*) Don't spill the liquor. None of the stuff from this bottle was ever burned over a pudding.

Lane "You're a gem, Lane," she'd say. She never had to ask for anything. I knew what was in her mind. I anticipated.

Cook To your good health and a better colour. (*She drinks*)

Lane "A jewel, aren't you, Lane?" she'd say. And we'd look at each other in her mirror. (*She empties her glass at a gulp*)

Cook That should do something for you. (*She takes the glass from Lane*)

Lane Black eyes, blazing back in the glass. Old women have faded eyes that water, but hers . . . they shone like burning coals.

Cook A jewel, eh? She'd never let you out of her clutches, then. No jewel ever slipped through *her* fingers.

Lane Those black eyes looked right inside you.

Cook So she wore the full collection at the end, eh? Every piece?

Lane Right through to the thoughts you hoped were hidden.

Cook Not more than one pair of ear-rings at a time, surely.

Lane Who can help what they're thinking?

Cook Though I suppose there were places where the rest might have dangled.

Lane Night after night as we handled the stones. What would you have thought about at such a time?

Cook Why should you be so uneasy now?

Lane Uneasy? "Blood and tears they cost," she'd say. "Nothing gleams like blood and tears."

Cook Well, they're listed and locked away. (*She replaces the brandy bottle and the glasses in the cupboard*)

Lane She knew what I was thinking. "Would you pay that price?" she'd say . . . Yes, they're locked away for safety.

Cook And listed, too. By you and Mrs Abernethy, you said.

Lane The lawyers will need a list. Mrs Abernethy writes a beautiful hand.

Cook There's education for you.

Lane I remembered every piece.

Cook Practice makes perfect. You handled every one as it went back into the box.
Lane For the last time.
Cook At least that's temptation out of the way.
Lane Why do you say that?
Cook You said she knew what you were thinking.
Lane I was thinking—every stone had its story. Mostly of wickedness.
Cook You didn't list the stories.
Lane They're best forgotten. Buried with her.
Cook If she had her way, the jewels would go the same road. She'd loose her grip on life sooner than she'd loose her grip on them.
Lane How can you imagine such nonsense?
Cook Don't you? I see what I see, and I speak my mind.
Lane Pepper and mustard are all very well in the kitchen; but a lady's maid has to learn discretion.

Footsteps are heard on the stairs, off

Footsteps on the stairs. You'll be discreet in front of the midwife, I hope. We don't want gossip in the village.
Cook Whatever's said here, there'll be gossip there.

Mrs Abernethy enters with the candle. She looks back and calls before Twilley has a chance to sneak past the opening

Mrs Abernethy In here, Twilley.

Twilley appears in the doorway

Twilley Just going to empty the water.
Mrs Abernethy Come into the kitchen.
Twilley Won't take but a minute.
Mrs Abernethy I told you to wait.

Twilley enters reluctantly, carrying a large bowl of water. She also carries a diamond ring, concealed in her hand

Throughout the following dialogue, Mrs Abernethy does not take her eyes from Twilley, even though this may mean talking to the others without looking at them. Twilley is equally anxious to escape

Twilley I've carried this water down four flights.
Mrs Abernethy Then set it on the floor. But don't stir a finger until I give you leave.

Twilley puts down her burden as Mrs Boone, a usually good-humoured rustic, waddles into the kitchen

Mrs Boone Running downstairs is a great game for them as knows the course; but it holds pitfalls for beginners who can't tell a twist from a turn.
Mrs Abernethy I held a candle.
Mrs Boone So far in front it acted like a jack o' lantern. I'm thankful to have my feet on solid flags again. A restorative wouldn't come amiss.
Cook You've done all that had to be done?
Mrs Boone All that can be done after the spark has flown—washed and shrouded, with pennies on her eyes. The poor lady was taken unawares, eh?
Lane We were all taken unawares.
Mrs Boone But her most of all, I reckon. Well, I've never been one for intruding on private grief . . .
Twilley I'll show you to the door.
Mrs Abernethy No, Twilley.
Mrs Boone At such times there are some as takes to stimulants, and some as prefers oblivion. Myself, I'm impartial between the teapot or the bottle: glad to settle for whatever turns up.
Mrs Abernethy Mrs Boone can show herself to the door.
Mrs Boone I'll own there's more welcome at a lying-in than a laying-out; but on both occasions I've come to expect certain —little obligings. Such as the second best tea service. Not a ceremony of the first importance, no—but a bit above your casual hospitality.
Mrs Abernethy You'll excuse our lack of ceremony tonight.
Twilley I'll fill the kettle.
Mrs Abernethy No, Twilley.
Mrs Boone Even teetotals offer tea.
Mrs Abernethy Take this candle. (*She holds out the candle*) You can leave it by the door.
Mrs Boone Put that way, I'll leave you too.
Mrs Abernethy Good night.
Twilley I can . . .
Mrs Abernethy No, Twilley.
Mrs Boone I wouldn't accept now if asked.

Mrs Boone takes the candle and sweeps out

Twilley I'll fetch the candle.
Mrs Abernethy No, Twilley.
Cook This is my kitchen, Mrs Abernethy. Perhaps you'll have the goodness...

Mrs Abernethy holds up a finger. There is the sound of a distant door being slammed

Mrs Abernethy Where is it, Twilley?
Lane Where is what?
Mrs Abernethy Twilley knows.
Twilley Don't know nothing, Mrs Abernethy. Never did.
Mrs Abernethy Hand it to me.
Twilley I haven't got nothing to hand.
Mrs Abernethy What would you have done with it if I'd let you out of my sight? Slipped it into your shoe? Hidden it under a mat? Swallowed it?
Twilley These are riddles, Mrs Abernethy.
Mrs Abernethy You know the answers. What did you pick up, Twilley?
Cook Pick up?
Twilley There wasn't nothing to pick up. Only this pancheon. There wasn't nothing else near the bed.
Mrs Abernethy Or under the bed, Twilley? Deep in the pile of the rug?
Twilley Anywhere. My goodness you'd have to be quick for that, and I'm not quick. Never was. "Too slow to let lice crawl off you," Cook says. I couldn't never take any advantage.
Mrs Abernethy I saw you.
Twilley You was turned away. Standing over *her*.
Mrs Abernethy A gleam in the candlelight—flashing across the mirror like a shooting star.
Twilley I didn't see nothing in the mirror.
Lane It wasn't...?
Mrs Abernethy What was it, Twilley? And what have you done with it?
Twilley Cross my heart.
Mrs Abernethy Show me, Twilley. Open your hand.

Twilley defiantly puts her hands behind her back

Twilley I ain't got nothing in my hands.

Who Calls?

Mrs Abernethy Hold them out. Both together.

Twilley surreptitiously drops the ring behind her and then holds out her hands

Twilley See. (*She advances triumphantly towards Mrs Abernethy, hands held out*)
Cook What was that?
Twilley I never had nothing to drop.

Cook crosses to where Twilley was standing and picks up the ring

Cook Twinkle. Twinkle.
Twilley I never found no ring.
Cook We're always sweeping diamond rings off this kitchen floor. Some careless folks round here, Mrs Abernethy.
Mrs Abernethy Lane and I removed her jewelry most carefully.
Lane It could hardly have been left on her to tempt the midwife.
Cook Temptation indeed. Why this could fetch . . .
Mrs Abernethy Who knows how it came to fall by the bed.
Cook Or how long it might have gone on lying if Twilley hadn't . . .
Twilley I never. I'm no thief. It were on the floor, then it were in my hand.
Cook With the Mistress lying so close. What would she have said if she'd known?
Twilley She wouldn't have said nothing.
Cook She treasured her little keepsakes. If she'd guessed, she'd have risen up and . . .
Twilley Don't say them things. I were going to give it up.
Mrs Abernethy Why didn't you?
Twilley I only wanted to hold it a little while. Maybe look at it, and fancy what it were like to have rings on your fingers. I wouldn't have kept it. What's to happen now?
Cook I expect it will join the other trinkets. Eh, Mrs Abernethy?
Mrs Abernethy What else?
Twilley I mean—what's to become of me?
Mrs Abernethy What indeed? We must consider.
Twilley I never thought.
Cook True, Twilley. Never.
Twilley I never stole. You know that. Mistress knew it.
Cook Perhaps that's why she didn't rise up, and . . .

Twilley Don't!

Cook Stop bawling and empty that water away. Yes, Mrs Abernethy?

Twilley Aye. (*She takes up the bowl*)

Cook Wash and dry it well afterwards.

Twilley exits

Cook closes the door after her

Mrs Abernethy The ring, Cook.

Cook Twilley didn't think. How could she, without the equipment?

Mrs Abernethy It has to be locked away with all the rest.

Cook I've been thinking, though. How came this pretty thing to be missed when everything was listed so carefully?

Lane If it dropped silently, unobserved . . .

Cook Put the other way—how came it *not* to be missed? You remembered all the others so clearly. With all their stories. This one spins a fine yarn all on its own.

Mrs Abernethy You've been at the brandy.

Cook I have indeed. Never tell a lie when the truth serves as well. But what have you been at?

Lane Aspersions?

Cook The Mistress ablaze with a royal ransom, Lane. Only you and her knows exactly how much. What if it didn't all find its way back into the jewel box? Who's to know? Who'd miss a sparkle or so?

Lane Is that an accusation?

Cook Who's proof against temptation? Not me, I admit. Not even Mrs Abernethy.

Mrs Abernethy So your insinuations extend to me. You forget your place, Cook.

Cook I don't have a place, Mrs Abernethy. No more than you, or Lane, or silly Twilley. Who pays wages when your employer's underground? It's back to the registries and the advertisements again . . . "Experienced Housekeeper", "Lady's Maid", 'Plain and Fancy Cook". And what do we live on between households?

Mrs Abernethy That is your problem.

Cook You've solved yours? The two of you were closeted for an hour before the doctor's pony and trap.

Who Calls?

Mrs Abernethy You're well aware of what we were about.
Cook Too true.
Mrs Abernethy Lane, you witnessed this slander.
Cook Witnessed more than that, I'll be bound. Whatever was done was done in a hurry. More haste less speed. How else came an item of such value to be overlooked?
Mrs Abernethy I warn you—if you repeat this monstrous fabrication . . .
Cook The fat would be in the fire, wouldn't it?
Lane We've not all been corrupted in our dealings with tradesmen. Yes, we all know about short weight, commissions, and a little extra on the bill. But some of us know what loyalty is.
Cook We all know what loyalty is. We all served that old bundle of corruption faithfully; but she's no more, and now our loyalties lie in different directions. Towards ourselves. Could that have been your line of reasoning, Mrs Abernethy?
Mrs Abernethy I deny it.
Cook No matter. We've reached the same conclusion. Here. (*She holds out the ring*)
Mrs Abernethy What . . . ?
Cook The ring, Mrs A. Take hold of it. Put it with the others.
Mrs Abernethy Add it to the rest?
Cook You know what I mean.
Mrs Abernethy A sudden conversion. (*She takes the ring*)
Cook Now we split three ways equal.
Lane No!
Cook You've no choice, Lane. Count that ring as my subscription to the general fund. It'll fetch a fair return at the right pawnshop. You won't be so much out at the final reckoning.
Mrs Abernethy I have agreed to nothing.
Cook Not in so many words. But there's no need for words where there's an understanding. We understand each other, my dears. Her up there—*she* understands us, too, I'm sure. She'd want to reward good and faithful service.

A bell rings. Slowly the trio look up at the line of bells

Lane She rang.
Cook I don't believe it.
Lane You heard.

Cook I still don't believe it.
Lane The bedroom bell. Her room.
Mrs Abernethy That room's empty.
Cook Except for *her*.
Lane Alone.
Cook She's dead.
Lane Is she?
Mrs Abernethy The doctor pronounced her dead. The midwife agreed.
Cook Could you have slipped the rings from her fingers while she lived?
Lane But her bell . . .
Mrs Abernethy We must be sensible. What's a bell? A thing at the end of a system of wires and pulleys. There's nothing mystical about a bell. It works according to mechanical principles. The system breaks and a bell shakes.
Lane A bell don't shake unless somebody shakes it.
Mrs Abernethy Anything touching a wire could move a bell.
Cook There you have it—a settling beam, wind under a board, a rat at the woodwork. Certainly not an old woman, lying at peace for the first time since she was a child.

The bell rings

Whatever moved it once could move it again.
Lane It's not natural.
Mrs Abernethy Whatever the cause it must be natural. We live in a scientific age. There must be an explanation if only we knew it.
Lane But what?
Mrs Abernethy Be satisfied there's an explanation somewhere.
Cook That's right. Be satisfied and forget it happened.
Lane But it did happen. She—she'll be expecting an answer.
Cook She didn't ring.
Lane The Mistress had one concern only—that when she rang, her call was answered. It always was answered. At once.
Cook We're too used to bells. Bells ring and we dance like dolls on wires.
Lane Who's to go up?
Mrs Abernethy Go up?
Cook Nobody's to go.

Who Calls?

Lane She'll be waiting.
Cook There's nobody up there. Nobody in the house but us three and Twilley.
Mrs Abernethy Twilley?
Cook Twilley!
Mrs Abernethy Could she have?
Cook She could. She's used to running up those stairs. She could be up them in a minute.
Mrs Abernethy You understand now. There had to be an explanation. It's Twilley. Only Twilley.
Lane Is this her idea of revenge?
Mrs Abernethy Oh, simple soul.
Cook I'll take a broomstick to her.

The bell rings. Cook shakes her fist at it

Pull the bell-rope, Twilley. That's right. Enjoy yourself. Before the reckoning. Are you laughing, Twilley?

Twilley enters, candle in hand

Twilley I'm not laughing, Cook. Should I be?
Cook Twilley? Here?
Lane It's not Twilley.
Twilley It's me all right, Miss Lane. What do you want?
Cook Shut the door and shut up.

Twilley does as she is bid, then stands irresolutely with the candle, wondering what to do next

Lane What's to be done now?
Cook Nothing.
Lane We must . . .
Cook Don't stir.
Lane Somebody must go.
Cook Why?
Lane Because the bell is always answered.
Cook Superstition.
Mrs Abernethy A bell *is* always answered.
Cook Even when there's nobody at the other end?
Lane If a bell rings, somebody must be there.
Cook Nobody we're answerable to.
Lane How are we to know?

Cook Because we're not answerable to anybody now.
Lane We always shall be. For us bells will always be ringing, and we'll always be answering them.
Cook Not in this house.
Mrs Abernethy Why not here as well as anywhere else?
Twilley (*for whom the penny has just dropped*) Did the bell ring?
Lane It did.
Mrs Abernethy Answer it, Twilley.
Twilley Me?
Mrs Abernethy You were engaged for that. To make up fires. To carry water. To trim the lamps. You are wanted in the Mistress's room.
Twilley There's no fire up there, and I just brought water down.
Mrs Abernethy If the bell rang, something is needed.
Twilley She's up there.
Mrs Abernethy She can't hurt anyone.
Twilley Did *she* ring the bell?
Mrs Abernethy How could she?
Twilley Then who did? What do you really want? You want to be rid of me again. Why? On account of the ring? I'm sorry I picked it up. I'll forget I ever saw it. If you want me out of the kitchen, I'll go and sit in the scullery. I don't mind the scullery. If you want me out of the kitchen why must I go to her room?
Lane Because the call came from her room.
Twilley It never. How could it?
Mrs Abernethy You can tell us, Twilley. When you come down.
Twilley You're the ones who heard it. Suppose it should be for you.
Cook Bring a message.
Twilley I'm to go up there?
Mrs Abernethy You're slow, Twilley.
Twilley I've always been slow.
Mrs Abernethy But not usually so slow.

Twilley does not move

You'll be needing a reference, Twilley. Very soon. Shall I write "Slow, but willing" or "Very slow and surly"?
Twilley I'm not willing. All them stairs and only one candle.
Mrs Abernethy Four candles are blazing in that room. I lit them

Who Calls?

all myself. You need only open the door, Twilley. If there is —no call for your services, then return.

Twilley If there's no call for my services, why must I go?

Mrs Abernethy Because we can't tell, can we, Twilley? Who is calling for what.

Twilley Must I?

Mrs Abernethy If you wish to leave here with any sort of character, you must. If you ever hope to enter service again, you must. If you don't wish to end in a ditch or the workhouse, you must.

Twilley Then I must. (*She moves towards the door slowly, muttering to keep up her courage*) I must. I must. I must . . .

She goes, closing the door behind her

There is a pause. The bell rings

Lane Why?

Mrs Abernethy Who knows? (*She opens her hand and looks at the ring*)

Lane That?

Cook And more?

Mrs Abernethy And more. Where your treasure is, there will be your heart also. So I was taught.

Lane Her heart was always with her treasure.

Cook You can't take it with you. That's what I was taught. Though I shouldn't be surprised at her trying.

Mrs Abernethy Should this be returned to the jewel box? Should the others be replaced?

Cook Should she be buried in full regalia—with a fortune glittering on her shroud?

Mrs Abernethy That would be a futile gesture, if not outright heathen.

Cook One gesture makes as much sense as the other. Who's to benefit from her treasure now? Strangers. She never owned to a family. Who ought to benefit? Who did most for her? Us, while she was here. Now she's gone . . .

Lane Has she?

Mrs Abernethy We both touched the body, already nearly cold.

Lane But her spirit. Where is that?

Cook In hell if there's any justice.

Lane What if . . .?

Cook I warned you about wasting money on penny romances. You've come to swallow that twaddle.

Mrs Abernethy All the same I fear . . .

Cook You, Mrs Abernethy? Never. You never feared a thing, except perhaps an unpaid bill.

Mrs Abernethy Tales have been told.

Cook What are stories? Rubbish grown on idleness.

Mrs Abernethy Of seeming dead who have returned.

Cook Name one.

Mrs Abernethy I've heard of a funeral service interrupted by a knocking. When the coffin lid was raised the occupant was found to be alive.

Cook Anybody we know?

Mrs Abernethy Such an occurrence is not beyond possibility.

Cook Seeing's believing.

Mrs Abernethy What if we were about to witness . . .

Cook You won't make my blood run cold, Mrs A.; but if you carry on like that you'll scare Lane into a fit. She's that white she'd pass for a corpse herself.

Mrs Abernethy What if that seeming death were a mere catalepsy?

Cook The Mistress is dead, Mrs A. We have the doctor's word for it. Long words won't bring her back.

Mrs Abernethy We must be practical, Cook—we three conspirators.

Lane Conspirators?

Mrs Abernethy What else? If the Mistress were to revive, what would be her first reaction?

Cook She'd loose a flood of language fouler than a tinker's. Then she'd ring.

Lane She'd ring.

Mrs Abernethy Being the Mistress where would her thoughts fly first?

Lane To her jewel box.

Mrs Abernethy Which was removed.

Cook For its own safety.

Mrs Abernethy She'll demand it.

Cook You've slipped from "would" to "will".

Mrs Abernethy We must be prepared.

Cook For miracles?

Mrs Abernethy Articles of value are no longer where they were. If she discovers their loss . . .

Cook She can't in her condition.

Mrs Abernethy If she should . . .

Cook It's a long road from "if" to "is".

Mrs Abernethy Perhaps we should . . .

Lane Yes. Now.

Cook No. I came late to this conspiracy, as you call it; but I'll have a voice in it. Once those jewels have been put back, you'll never have the courage to take 'em again. You grabbed them on impulse. Once they're in their box again, you'll dicker and dicker until lawyers have taken possession.

Lane They belong to her.

Cook They did while she was alive.

Mrs Abernethy She may be alive still.

Cook She's not.

Lane Then who rang the bell?

Cook Ah. Ah, yes. Why—Twilley will tell us.

The door opens a crack and Twilley slips in. She stands, blinking nervously

Well?

Mrs Abernethy You saw the Mistress?

Twilley nods

Lane Was she as you saw her last?

Twilley nods

Mrs Abernethy You saw clearly? Were the candles still burning?

Twilley nods

Lane Were her eyes closed?

Twilley nods

Mrs Abernethy The hands folded?

Twilley nods

Lane Were her cheeks as waxy? Still without colour?

Twilley nods

Mrs Abernethy Had she moved?

Twilley shakes her head

Lane No part of her?

Twilley shakes her head

Mrs Abernethy Her head. The clothes. Her lips?

Twilley shakes her head

Lane No sign of life?

Twilley shakes her head

Mrs Abernethy Thank you, Twilley.
Cook So there's no more to be said.
Mrs Abernethy Nothing more to discuss.
Cook The—articles in question stay where they are?
Mrs Abernethy Agreed.
Lane Questions won't go away. Such as who or how or what? If one answer wasn't right we ought to look for another.
Cook We'll do no such thing.
Mrs Abernethy I suggest we retire.
Lane To bed?
Mrs Abernethy The day has been full of incident and tomorrow's load may well be heavier. Undertakers. Attorneys. We shall need all our wits. Now we need sleep.
Lane Can we sleep with *her* in the house?
Cook Are you going to stay awake until after the funeral? Three days without sleep and you'll see ghosts in earnest.
Lane If ever a spirit was earthbound, hers would be.
Cook "If" again. Confound your "ifs".
Lane She'll not loose hold so easily.
Cook None of us is given the option. "Naked I came: naked I go", if you'll pardon the preacher's expression.
Mrs Abernethy When one is called, one is called.
Cook She was called sudden, but she went.
Lane But what's calling now? What draws her? The likes of that ring?

Twilley gives a little cry. During the next few speeches panic mounts in her

Mrs Abernethy You forget yourself, Lane. You forget whose company we are sharing.

Cook Blabber at that rate, and it's not only company we'll have to share.

Mrs Abernethy That will suffice, Cook. Observe the decencies. In a house of mourning we preserve an atmosphere of calm. We speak—when we have to speak—in such tones as befit the occasion. I shall order lilies tomorrow. I believe the Mistress would have wished it so.

Lane What happened—happened.

Mrs Abernethy Nothing happened. A minor fault in the communication system. It has not been repeated. Set an example to the lower orders, Lane. We had only one fear—an outlandish possibility, which Twilley has dispelled.

Twilley begins to cry

See how infectious hysteria can become. Now Twilley loses control. Stolid, thick-skinned Twilley, who has just seen the Mistress at peace.

Twilley She hasn't.

Cook What?

Twilley I didn't see no Mistress.

Mrs Abernethy But you told us . . .

Twilley I didn't dare go up.

Cook You lied!

Twilley I turned round at the bottom of the stairs. Then I waited outside the door 'til it seemed as though there'd been time to get back.

Mrs Abernethy You're dismissed!

Twilley I couldn't do it.

Mrs Abernethy As from this instant.

Twilley I told myself I had to, but my feet wouldn't move.

Mrs Abernethy Insubordination.

Twilley Not after hearing the other feet.

Lane After . . . ?

Mrs Abernethy Other?

Twilley Up above.

Cook A board creaked. Boards are always creaking.

Twilley Boards don't slip an' slither. Slip and slither, feeling their way. Slip and slither. On the stairs.

Mrs Abernethy You heard . . . ?
Lane She heard.

The door is flung open with a crash, and an Intruder (the Mistress) stands framed in it, eyes blazing

Mistress Thieves! Thieves! Thieves!

Lane screams and covers her face. The Mistress points accusingly at Mrs Abernethy

Traitors!
Twilley The ring! She's come back for the ring.
Mistress The rest. The rest.
Twilley Give it her, and let her go.
Mistress Where? Where?
Lane (*babbling*) They weren't stolen. They were taken for safety. They'll be returned. We promise. You'll have them. Every pin. Every brooch. Everything we took.
Mistress You . . . you . . .
Lane Not only me. All of them.
Mistress All? All?
Mrs Abernethy Heaven forgive me.

The Mistress gives a wild shriek and staggers towards Mrs Abernethy, arms outstretched and fingers crooked. At the last step, however, she falters. Her voice dies to a moan, and she crumples to the floor. There is silence. Cook kneels by the body

The doctor . . .
Cook No need. She's quite cold.
Mrs Abernethy She stood at the door.
Lane She knew. She knew what we'd taken. Is there a fury strong enough to raise the dead?
Cook Who knows? But she can't lie there.
Twilley She said . . .
Cook Twilley, give a hand.
Twilley Everything we took, she said.
Cook You misunderstood.
Twilley Twilley's slow, but Twilley understood.
Cook When you come for a character . . .
Twilley I reckon I've as much character as anybody here. How much was took? No matter. I want a share.

LIGHTING PLOT

Property fittings required: lamp, candles, well-stoked range (optional)
Interior. A kitchen

To open: Night. Dim, shadowy lighting. Red glow from range
No cues

EFFECTS PLOT

Cue 1	**Cook:** " . . . listening for that bell." *Bell rings*	(Page 3)
Cue 2	**Lane:** " . . . has to learn discretion." *Footsteps on the stairs, off*	(Page 6)
Cue 3	**Cook:** " . . . you'll have the goodness . . ." *Pause then distant door slam*	(Page 8)
Cue 4	**Cook:** " . . . good and faithful service." *Bell rings*	(Page 11)
Cue 5	**Cook:** " . . . since she was a child." *Bell rings*	(Page 12)
Cue 6	**Cook:** " . . . broomstick to her." *Bell rings*	(Page 13)
Cue 7	**Twilley** exits *Pause, then bell rings*	(Page 15)
Cue 8	**Mrs Abernethy:** " . . . yet to be calculated, Twilley." *Bell rings*	(Page 21)
Cue 9	**Mrs Abernethy:** " . . . yet to be paid." *Bell rings*	(Page 21)

MADE AND PRINTED IN GREAT BRITAIN BY
LATIMER TREND & COMPANY LTD PLYMOUTH
MADE IN ENGAND

Mrs Abernethy A share in what?
Twilley In everything, Mrs Abernethy.
Lane Think what you're asking, Twilley.
Twilley I know what I want.
Mrs Abernethy You shall have it.
Twilley What will a fourth share in everything come to?
Mrs Abernethy The price has yet to be calculated, Twilley.

The bell rings. Twilley reacts

Lane You heard?
Twilley I heard.
Mrs Abernethy Who knows what has yet to be paid.

The bell rings. Twilley puts her hands over her ears

Who knows?

                        CURTAIN

FURNITURE AND PROPERTY LIST

The following plot lists essential furniture. Further dressing may be added at the producer's discretion.

On stage: 4 chairs
Cupboard. *In it:* candles, bottle of brandy, 2 glasses

Off stage: Bowl of water **(Twilley)**
Diamond ring **(Twilley)**

28. SEP. 1983		
-8. JUN. 1984		
5 JULY 1984		
30 JULY		
8 SEPT 84		
-6 MAR 1985		
20 JUN		
11 JAN 1989		

	ACC. No.	DY28299
CAMPTON	Who calls	5

ESSEX COUNTY LIBRARY
H.Q. BIB: SERVICES
.... LIBRARY

This book is to be returned on or before the last date above.

It may be borrowed for a further period if not in demand.